Cambridge **Discovery Education**™

▶ **INTERACTIVE READERS**

Series editor: Bob Hastings

WATER POWER
THE GREATEST FORCE ON EARTH

B2

Karmel Shreyer

CAMBRIDGE
UNIVERSITY PRESS

Discovery
EDUCATION™

CAMBRIDGE UNIVERSITY PRESS
Cambridge, New York, Melbourne, Madrid, Cape Town,
Singapore, São Paulo, Delhi, Mexico City

Cambridge University Press
32 Avenue of the Americas, New York, NY 10013-2473, USA

www.cambridge.org
Information on this title: www.cambridge.org/9781107688971

First published 2014

Printed in Hong Kong, China, by Golden Cup Printing Company Limited

A catalog record for this publication is available from the British Library.

Library of Congress Cataloging-in-Publication Data

Schreyer, Karmel.
  Water power : the greatest force on earth / Karmel Schreyer.
    pages cm. -- (Cambridge discovery interactive readers)
  ISBN 978-1-107-68897-1 (pbk. : alk. paper)
  1. Water-power--Juvenile literature. 2. English language--Textbooks for foreign speakers.
  3. Readers (Elementary) I. Title.

TC146.S38 2013
333.91'4--dc23

2013018627

ISBN 978-1-107-68897-1

Additional resources for this publication at www.cambridge.org

Layout services, art direction, book design, and photo research: Q2ABillSMITH GROUP
Editorial services: Hyphen S.A.
Audio production: CityVox, New York
Video production: Q2ABillSMITH GROUP

Contents

Before You Read:
Get Ready!

Water – we need it, but it causes problems for us, too. Throughout history, we have found ways to use water for our benefit. But even today, can we really control the amazing power of water?

Words to Know

Complete the sentences with the correct words.

dam

drought

erosion

irrigation

1 Centuries ago, humans created a way to water fields easily, with _____ systems.

2 A _____ is a strong wall built across a river to stop the water or make a lake.

3 When there is no rain in a place for a long time, there is a _____ .

4 Heavy rain can wash away the land and cause _____ .

Non-renewable energy sources can only be used once and are difficult to replace. Renewable energy sources can be used again and are easily replaced. Are these energy sources non-renewable or renewable? Complete the chart below.

coal

geothermal energy

hydroelectric energy

natural gas

nuclear energy

oil

solar energy

wind energy

Non-renewable energy sources	Renewable energy sources
❶ _____	❹ _____
❷ _____	❺ _____
❸ _____	❻ _____
	❼ _____
	❽ _____

CHAPTER 1

Water on Earth

IT IS NO SURPRISE WE CALL THE EARTH "THE BLUE PLANET". AFTER ALL, OVER 60 PERCENT OF ITS SURFACE IS COVERED WITH WATER.

It is water that gives Earth its beautiful blue color that we see in photographs taken from space. No other planet that we know of in the universe has so much water, that amazing element so essential to life.

Water goes through a cycle that never ends. It falls from the sky as rain and snow, sleet,[1] and hail.[2] On high mountains, **glaciers** melt and water flows from narrow streams and wide rivers into lakes and eventually into the seas and oceans. Then, through a process called **evaporation**, water rises from the seas to the skies where it turns into clouds. And the cycle begins again. Water can be liquid, solid, or gas; it can be gentle or rough; it can bring life or death.

[1]**sleet:** a mixture of snow and rain
[2]**hail:** small, hard balls of ice that fall from the sky like rain

Water has power over us – maybe more than anything else on the planet! Without water, no human, animal, or plant could survive. Humans have long used water for washing, growing food, and raising animals. Water has also been used as a means of transportation, as a source of recreation, and as a household tool. Now, we also use water as an industrial tool and as a **source** of energy.

But too much water can be a bad and dangerous thing. Think of floods, for example. Fast-moving, deep water can drown[3] people; it can sweep away vehicles and even buildings. Also, floodwater may contain bacteria that cause diseases and that can affect our drinking water.

Water gives us power, but it also has power over us.

[3]**drown:** die because you are under water and cannot breathe

Video Quest

Life Support System

Watch this video and say how you think water will be used in the future.

CHAPTER 2

Water in Industry

THE AMOUNT OF WATER USED IN INDUSTRY IS GROWING STEADILY EACH YEAR. AS MORE COUNTRIES DEVELOP ECONOMICALLY, MORE WATER WILL BE NEEDED FOR INDUSTRIAL USE.

Water is important in industry. In fact, about 20 percent of all the water we use around the world is for industrial purposes.

We need water in every step of the industrial process. For example, sometimes water is needed in the production of food items like soft drinks, soups, and juices. And we also need it for things like soap, shampoo, paint, and cleaning liquids. But did you know that water is required for the production of plastic and glass? Water is even used when making cars! It takes about 2,000 liters of water to make one car tire! It sounds unbelievable, but it's true.

We need tools to make things, and water can also be used as a tool. For example, water is often used to cut things.

When a line or jet of water is shot out at a high speed and under high pressure, it can be very strong – strong enough to cut through glass, metal, and stone. Because of this, water jet cutting machines are used in industries like mining and aerospace to cut things to the right shape. Water jets are also used at the dentist's office to help us keep our teeth clean. Fortunately, they're not as strong as the ones used to cut stone or metal!

Water is also used in industry as a lubricant – something that can help prevent machines from wearing out when their parts move against each other. Right now, most industrial lubricants are made with oil, but because using oil in this way is not good for the environment, inventors are developing water-based lubricants.

Because water is inexpensive and easy to get, it is also used as a coolant – to cool down the moving parts of machines in factories and power plants.

A water jet cutting machine

? APPLY

Think of a case of water pollution caused by industry. What happened?

Water is also used to move things where they need to go. Trees are cut down and floated along rivers from faraway forests, for example. It would be hard, in fact, for trade to exist without water as a means of transportation.

Shipping is a huge industry that helps us move the things we make around the world as cheaply as possible. And water is also used to transport waste – including human waste! – to waste-treatment facilities, where it is diluted,[4] broken down, and dealt with safely.

[4]**dilute:** make a liquid thinner by adding another liquid to it, such as water

Water is also used to create the power we need to keep our industries running. Hydroelectric generating[5] plants use the energy of falling water to turn turbines, which then create electricity. This electricity is taken to cities and towns along power lines.

Without water, most industrial work would be more dangerous, more expensive, and, in some cases, impossible. But there are problems. For example, industrial processes may cause pollution. Dangerous chemicals can pollute the water, harm people, and damage the environment.

[5]**generate:** make energy

CHAPTER 3

Falling Water

WATER POWER – HYDROPOWER – IS ALMOST MAGICAL! IMAGINE, POWER CREATED FROM THE ENERGY OF FALLING WATER.

When the energy from large amounts of falling water is captured,[6] it can be used for many practical purposes.

From as early as the 6th century BCE, the ancient Egyptians used the power of falling water to create a system to water their fields and gardens easily. This is a process called irrigation.

Other ancient civilizations in China and Persia also developed complex irrigation systems, made up of wells,[7] dams, and canals. These irrigation systems made use of the natural power of **gravity** to move the water from higher to lower land and to send water into places to keep it for later use.

[6]**capture:** catch or collect something so you can use it later

[7]**well:** a deep hole in the ground from which you can get water, oil, or gas

Water power was also used as a way to tell time, by measuring how much water flowed into or out of a vessel.[8] Water clocks were first used in ancient Egypt and Babylon around the 14th century BCE. Over the centuries, water clocks became increasingly complex machines.

The water wheel was invented by the Ancient Greeks around the 1st century BCE. The water wheel used the energy of flowing or falling water to power other machinery, and it had many important uses. For example, water wheels were used in mills to turn wheat into flour and to press wood into pulp for making paper. This hard work didn't have to be done by animals or people anymore.

Centuries later, the water wheel was still in use in sawmills to cut wood and in factories to make cloth. It wasn't until the invention of **steam**-powered machinery and electricity that the water wheel was replaced by more efficient machines.

A mill

[8] **vessel:** a container, such as a bottle or jar

The next great improvement in water power was in the 19th century, when the modern water turbine was invented. The turbine was a kind of engine that used the energy of moving water to create power for industrial use. And this turbine design was improved over the years, making it a very efficient machine for powering industry.

At the end of the 19th century, two important things happened. First, hydroelectricity was developed: electricity could be generated from water power. Second, a way was invented to take this electricity over long distances, along power lines.

By the early 20th century, hydroelectric power plants, which included dams, were being built on rivers all over the United States. The famous Hoover Dam, on the Colorado River, was completed in 1936. Today, hydroelectric power is the most common form of **renewable energy** in the world!

Hydroelectric power is relatively cheap, and unlike power plants that burn non-renewable resources like coal, hydroelectric power doesn't directly cause air pollution. But there are still some problems.

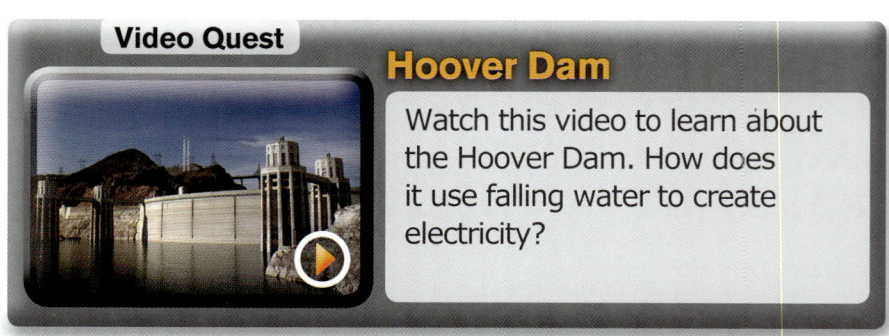

Video Quest

Hoover Dam

Watch this video to learn about the Hoover Dam. How does it use falling water to create electricity?

For example, when a dam is built as part of a hydroelectric power plant, the environment, including plant and animal life is affected. Hydroelectric power is not the perfect solution to our energy problems.

An interesting idea for water power involves storing[9] the power from other renewable energy sources, such as wind turbines, when more power is generated than is needed at a particular time. This can be done by pumping[10] water up a mountain to a reservoir[11] and storing it there. Then, when power is needed, the water is let out of the reservoir so it can generate hydroelectricity.

[9] **store:** put something somewhere and not use it until you need it
[10] **pump:** move a liquid with a machine
[11] **reservoir:** a place where water is kept before it goes to people's houses

The Cruachan Dam in Scotland is a pumped storage hydroelectric plant.

CHAPTER 4

Steam

STEAM IS PRODUCED WHEN WATER IS HEATED TO ITS BOILING POINT, 100° CELSIUS.

Steam is a source of water power, too! Remember that water can exist in three forms: liquid (water), solid (ice), or gas (steam). When water changes from a liquid to a gas, it increases in volume by 1,600 times. This change creates a powerful force, or pressure, which can then become a source of power for machines.

In the 19th century the invention of the steam engine and steam turbine helped power the Industrial Revolution. This brought a great increase in all sorts of industrial activity and in the quantity of products for people to buy and sell. Without the power of water and steam, this would not have been possible.

A steam locomotive

Steam power also contributed to the settlement[12] of the American West by Europeans, which happened at about the same time as the Industrial Revolution. Thanks to the steam locomotive, large quantities of products and people could be transported long distances by train.

To power the locomotives, coal or wood was used to boil water. The resulting steam turned the wheels of the locomotive.

----

[12]**settlement:** when people start a town in a new place

An internal combustion engine

It's hard to believe, but steam was also used to power automobiles. In France, around the end of the 19th century, a steam-powered vehicle was invented by Amédée Bollée. This light steam car carried up to 12 people and moved at almost 60 kilometers per hour. Before World War I, the steam car was the most popular kind of car available. It was fast and quiet, too.

At the very same time, another kind of engine, the internal combustion engine, was being developed and perfected. By 1920, the steam engine and the steam car were considered old-fashioned. The internal combustion engine, driven by oil, had won the battle to power the automobile. The steam car was dead!

Steam is still used in our homes, though. We use steam-powered machines to clean carpets, to wash dishes, to cook food, and to heat our homes. Steam baths are very popular, too, especially in places like Finland and Japan.

While steam may no longer be considered a useful way to power industry, trains, or automobiles, it may still be an important source of energy if we can think of how to use it more efficiently. These days, we are all very concerned about the negative effects of non-renewable energy forms such as oil and gas on our environment. Steam is now being looked at as a potential renewable resource – in the form of geothermal energy.

Geothermal energy is energy which comes from heat generated deep inside the Earth. This source of power is popular in places where there is a lot of geothermal activity, like Iceland.

By using our power of invention, in places where steam is naturally available, we can find ways to use it to provide the energy power we need.

ANALYZE

What are some of the ways water power has been used to improve the quality of modern life?

Steam rises from the ground in Krýsuvík, Iceland.

CHAPTER 5

The Downside of Water Power

THROUGHOUT HISTORY, PEOPLE HAVE FOUND WAYS TO USE WATER FOR OUR BENEFIT. BUT, SOMETIMES, THE POWER OF WATER WORKS AGAINST US.

When water flows over land, little by little it breaks apart the rock and soil[13] and moves them away. This erosion of the ground can destroy buildings, roads, and railways built near water. Erosion can change the direction of rivers, too, and that can lead to international problems. In the early 1960s, the Chamizal Dispute between Mexico and the United States occurred when a change in river flow made a large island in the middle of the Rio Grande, the border between Mexico and Texas.

[13]**soil:** the top part of the land where plants grow

Video Quest

Erosion

Watch the video to learn more about erosion. How can water affect the natural landscape?

Water power can cause natural disasters. Flooding can occur naturally when mountain snow melts in the springtime or heavy seasonal rains cause rivers to overflow.

But flooding can also be the result of human activity, like when a dam breaks. In 2005, the dams holding back the water of the Gulf of Mexico were destroyed by Hurricane Katrina. New Orleans was flooded and more than a thousand people were killed.

Tsunami is a Japanese word, but now we all know what it means. In 2011, northeast Japan's coastal region was hit by giant waves of water after an earthquake occurred under the ocean floor.

Entire towns were destroyed, and a nuclear **power plant** was damaged. The plant was shut down, and thousands of people were moved to safety to avoid the risk of injury by **radioactivity**.

Avalanches are another example of the dangerous force of water in its solid form, as snow and ice. Avalanches occur when large quantities of snow fall down a mountain or hillside. Avalanches can bury skiers and buildings – and sometimes whole villages!

Too much water can cause disasters, but so can a lack of water. A drought occurs when there is not enough water, and it can be as serious a problem as flooding, maybe more serious.

Each year, millions of people around the world are affected by water shortages and droughts. Many people in poor countries die each year either from a lack of water or from polluted water. In wealthy countries, water shortages can result in crop failures. When this happens, food prices increase, causing problems of a different kind.

And finally, in the future there may be the problem of water wars. As clean water becomes less available, people may start to fight for it. Imagine not having safe, clean water flowing from your faucet or shower – no easy access to water to drink, to cook with, to wash, or to clean your clothes. Humans need water to survive. If one day it becomes a less plentiful resource, we may have a terrible crisis on our hands.

CHAPTER 6

What Do You Think?

NOWADAYS, THERE ARE MANY ISSUES FORMING AROUND WATER AND HOW WE USE IT, AND THESE ISSUES ARE VERY CONTROVERSIAL.

Water issues are the cause of a lot of debate. For example, while some people insist that we must make water conservation a priority, others believe that we must take advantage of what water can do for us. It is a source of energy for industry, which gives people jobs and income.

Water – we can't live without it, and yet, we waste it. Many people in richer countries around the world use as much water to flush[14] the toilet daily (as much as 20 liters) as people in poorer countries use for drinking, washing, and cooking each day. What can we do to stop wasting water?

[14]**flush:** clean something, especially a toilet, by sending water through it

24

Australia has recently suffered from a severe drought. A solution that the Australians have thought of to help save water is one that can easily be done at home – the shower timer! Instead of spending a long time in the shower, many people now set a shower timer to exactly four minutes. Even this small change has dramatically contributed to people's awareness of the need to save water.

Modern dishwashers also now use less water than washing dishes by hand, and modern toilets have a low-flush system that dramatically reduces the water wasted with each flush. What are some other ways people can save water at home? How many can you think of?

After You Read

Read the following sentences and choose Ⓐ, Ⓑ, Ⓒ, or Ⓓ.

1 How much of the Earth's surface is covered by water?

Ⓐ 25 percent
Ⓑ 50 percent
Ⓒ 60 percent
Ⓓ 80 percent

2 Which word does not belong?

Ⓐ rain
Ⓑ soil
Ⓒ sleet
Ⓓ hail

3 Which is <u>not</u> a use of water in industry?

Ⓐ coolant
Ⓑ sweetener
Ⓒ lubricant
Ⓓ tool

4 Which of the following was <u>not</u> needed for an ancient irrigation system?

Ⓐ dams
Ⓑ canals
Ⓒ gravity
Ⓓ evaporation

5 What resulted in steam-powered cars becoming old-fashioned?

Ⓐ improvements to the steam engine
Ⓑ improvements to the internal combustion engine
Ⓒ improvements in geothermal energy
Ⓓ improvements in road building

6 How is steam still used today in places like Iceland?

- (A) as hydroelectric energy
- (B) as nuclear energy
- (C) as geothermal energy
- (D) as internal combustion energy

7 Which is not an example of a disaster caused by water?

- (A) drought
- (B) tsunami
- (C) flooding
- (D) radioactivity

8 Droughts sometimes result in which of these things?

- (A) crop failure
- (B) steam turbines
- (C) tsunamis
- (D) avalanches

Text completion

Complete this news report with the correct words from the box.

flooding	nuclear	radiation	tsunami

On March 11, 2011, there was a big earthquake off the coast of northeastern Japan. This resulted in a large

1 _____ hitting the coast afterwards. The water forced its way onto the land, **2** _____ a lot of farmland, towns, and cities. It damaged the **3** _____ power plant in the city of Fukushima. People whose homes had not been destroyed by the disaster moved away to avoid the danger of

4 _____ .

Answer Key

Words to Know, page 4
1 irrigation **2** dam **3** drought **4** erosion

Words to Know, page 5
Non-renewable: coal, natural gas, oil
Renewable: geothermal, hydroelectric, nuclear, solar, wind

Video Quest, page 7
Answers will vary.

Apply, page 10
Answers will vary.

Video Quest, page 14
The dam collects water at a high level. The water runs down and is squeezed through pipes. The fast-moving water turns a turbine, and this creates an electric charge. This power is transported to cities along power lines.

Analyze, page 19
Answers will vary.

Video Quest, page 20
Water cuts through the land, which can result in strange and beautiful natural formations like the Grand Canyon.

Choose the Correct Answers, page 26
1 C **2** B **3** B **4** D **5** B **6** C **7** D **8** A

Text completion, page 27
1 tsunami **2** flooding **3** nuclear **4** radioactivity